Follow the Dollar

Dona Herweck Rice

Reader Consultants

Jennifer M. Lopez, M.S.Ed., NBCT
Senior Coordinator—History/Social Studies
Norfolk Public Schools

Tina Ristau, M.A., SLMS
Teacher Librarian
Waterloo Community School District

iCivics Consultants

Emma Humphries, Ph.D.
Chief Education Officer

Taylor Davis, M.T.
Director of Curriculum and Content

Natacha Scott, MAT
Director of Educator Engagement

Publishing Credits

Rachelle Cracchiolo, M.S.Ed., *Publisher*
Emily R. Smith, M.A.Ed., *VP of Content Development*
Véronique Bos, *Creative Director*
Dona Herweck Rice, *Senior Content Manager*
Dani Neiley, *Associate Content Specialist*
Fabiola Sepulveda, *Series Designer*

Image Credits: pp 11, 17 National Numismatic Collection, National Museum of American History; all other images from iStock and/or Shutterstock.

Library of Congress Cataloging-in-Publication Data

Names: Rice, Dona, author.
Title: Follow that dollar / Dona Herweck Rice.
Description: Huntington Beach, CA : Teacher Created Materials, [2021] | Includes index. | Audience: Grades 2-3 | Summary: "Every dollar has a story to tell. It travels from person to person or place to place. It is used to buy, pay, save, or share as it travels. It does this again and again and again. Where is it going next?"-- Provided by publisher.
Identifiers: LCCN 2020043570 (print) | LCCN 2020043571 (ebook) | ISBN 9781087605012 (paperback) | ISBN 9781087620039 (ebook)
Subjects: LCSH: Money--United States--Juvenile literature. | Dollar, American--Juvenile literature.
Classification: LCC HG221.5 .R528 2021 (print) | LCC HG221.5 (ebook) | DDC 332.4/973--dc23
LC record available at https://lccn.loc.gov/2020043570
LC ebook record available at https://lccn.loc.gov/2020043571

5482 Argosy Avenue
Huntington Beach, CA 92649-1039
www.tcmpub.com

ISBN 978-1-0876-0501-2
© 2022 Teacher Created Materials, Inc.

Table of Contents

The Dollar

A **dollar** may seem like just a piece of paper. But it stands for something bigger.

Dollars are important. They are the heart of the American **economy**. The economy is built on dollars earned, paid, saved, and spent.

Each person who lives in the country is part of the economy. People who visit the country are part of it too.

It can be fun to think about the path a dollar follows. Each dollar has a story to tell. Following its path can teach about the economy.

Jump into Fiction

The Money Tree

"Money doesn't grow on trees," Mom said when I asked her for a dollar to buy a candy bar. But then I asked her if I could spend a dollar I had earned to buy the candy. She said I could. I paid my dollar to the clerk in the store.

Just then, I remembered that it was my teacher's birthday the next day. I decided to give her the candy bar. She smiled so big and said, "You made my day!" I'm pretty sure she meant it!

A week later, my teacher brought cupcakes for the entire class! She used her dollars to buy them. She said that my gift inspired her, and she wanted to treat us all to a tasty surprise. The cupcakes were delicious. They were strawberry, my favorite.

CUPCAKES!!

Mom is right that money does not grow on trees. But I think the dollar I spent grew cupcakes!

Back to Nonfiction

A New Dollar

Imagine this. Your uncle hands you a crisp new dollar bill. It has come straight from the **mint** to the bank, where your uncle got it. You thank him and put the bill in your pocket.

You start to think about all the things you can spend it on. Your uncle reminds you that dollars are not just for spending but can be saved or shared as well. You decide that you really want to spend it!

First Dollar

The first U.S. dollar was printed in 1862. Abraham Lincoln was president then.

first U.S. dollar

You and your uncle walk to the discount store. You know you could buy many things for a dollar there. You just need to decide what has the best **value**.

A yo-yo catches your eye. It seems like a good deal. You could have hours of fun for just one dollar spent.

You give the dollar to the **cashier**. The yo-yo plus **tax** costs exactly one dollar! The cashier puts the bill in the **cash register**, and you leave to play with your new toy.

Think and Talk

Why might money be sorted like it is in the cash register here?

The Dollar Travels On

Every dollar ever made goes on a journey. It goes from person to person (or business). The story of you and your uncle could easily be true. Dollars travel in just this way.

Let's follow that same dollar. Imagine a man is behind you in line at the cash register. He gets a dollar in change for his purchase. It was your dollar.

On the street, the man stops at a newsstand to buy gum. He pays with his new dollar bill.

Baby of the Family

There is no bill in the U.S. economy smaller than the dollar. It is equal to 100 cents.

The newsstand owner decides it is time for a coffee break. He takes the dollar from his register. Then, he locks up the stand and walks to the coffee shop.

At the shop, the owner pays for his coffee using an **app** on his smartphone. There are many things he can pay for in this way. But he also spends his dollar. He leaves it in the **tip** jar for the **barista**.

There You Are, George!

George Washington was not always on the dollar bill. He first appeared on it in 1869.

After work, the barista takes her tips. Then, she walks home. Her son and his babysitter greet her. The barista pays the sitter. She uses dollars from her tip jar. The dollar you used at the discount store is one of them.

No Copies!

Dollar bills are hard to copy. Special ink, designs, and materials are used. This is so people will have a hard time making fake money look real.

So far, that dollar has gone from the mint to the sitter with seven stops in between. Each time it moves, people use it in a unique way. But the dollar always keeps its same value. That never changes.

Back Home

The dollar is almost like a piece on a gameboard that stays in play. There are many moves that can be made next. In this version, the sitter goes home with her dollars. Her home is your home. She is your big sister!

She counts her dollars and puts them in a box she keeps under her bed. The next day, she plans to make a deposit at the bank.

Dollar Coins

There are five different types of dollar coins made today. Each one equals one dollar.

She also wants to donate some of her money. The town's food bank feeds people in need. So, she wants to give to this cause. As part of the community, giving to those in need is a good thing to do.

PLEASE
DONATE

So, your sister puts some dollars in her savings account at the bank. She donates the rest to the food bank. The dollar you used at the store now belongs to the food bank. It helps to buy food and other supplies.

Dollar Strong

Dollars are most useful when they are on the move, just like the one in this book. People who earn and spend help an economy stay strong. If people just kept their dollars in boxes under their beds, the economy would stop moving. Dollars going from hand to hand keep things flowing. Of course, savings are a good thing too.

The next time you hold a dollar, think about its journey. Where has it been? Where is it going? If it could talk, what stories would the dollar have to tell?

Think and Talk

How can dollars on the move help the economy?

Glossary

app—a computer program

barista—a coffee maker and seller

cash register—a machine used in stores that adds customers' charges, makes change, and stores money

cashier—a person whose job is to take and give out money

dollar—the basic unit of money in the United States

economy—the system in a country or other area in which goods and services are bought and sold

mint—a place where money is made

tax—money collected by the government to pay for things used by the public and for government operations

tip—extra amount of money paid to a worker for services done

value—worth

Index

Civics in Action

Saving is part of supporting a strong economy. You may be able to save for things that cost more than you have now. Knowing how and when to save is a great skill to have!

1. Think of something you would like to buy.

2. Make a plan to buy this item. How can you save? How will you earn the money? How long will it take?

3. Think about if the item is worth the time and money it will take to buy it.

4. If you can, move forward with your plan. Save until you can buy. Or save until you decide you don't want it anymore!